The Library of SPIDERS™

Fishing Spiders

JAKE MILLER

The Rosen Publishing Group's

Published in 2004 by The Rosen Publishing Group, Inc.
29 East 21st Street, New York, NY 10010

First Edition

Editor: Jannell Khu
Book Design: Emily Muschinske
Layout Design: Nick Sciacca
Photo Research: Emily Muschinske

Photo Credits: Cover and pp. 1, 9 © Joe McDonald/Corbis; pp. 5, 9 (top), 13 (right), 17 © David Liebman; p. 6 George McCarthy/Corbis; p. 10 © Malcolm Kitto; Papillo/Corbis; p. 13 (left) © Carol Hughes; Gallo Images/Corbis; p. 14 © Royalty Free Corbis; p. 18 © Kelly C. Kissane & Bill Kositzky; p. 18 (inset) © Peggy Heard; Frank Lane Picture Agency/Corbis; p. 21 James L. Amos/Corbis; p. 21 (inset) © Hal Horowitz/Corbis.

Miller, Jake, 1969–
Fishing spiders / Jake Miller.
     v. cm. — (The Library of spiders)
Includes bibliographical references (p.   ).
Contents: The fishing spider — The fishing spider's family — The fishing spider's body — Walking on water — How fishing spiders hunt — The nursery web — The fishing spider's eggs — Baby fishing spiders — The fishing spider's enemies — Fishing spiders and people.
ISBN 0-8239-6711-5 (lib. bdg.)
1. Dolomedes—Juvenile literature. [1. Fisher spiders. 2. Spiders.] I. Title. II. Series.
QL458.42.P5 M55 2004
595.4'4—dc21

                              2002014773

Manufactured in the United States of America

Contents

The Fishing Spider

On the edges of ponds, streams, and swamps throughout the world, huge spiders the size of a small child's hand wait for **prey**. These large, hairy spiders are called fishing spiders. Fishing spiders got their name because they hunt small fish, frogs, **tadpoles**, lizards, and insects that live in and around water. Fishing spiders can run, jump, and row across the surface of the water. They move quickly and are strong enough to pull a small fish or a frog out of the water and carry it to the shore!

Fishing spiders use their front legs to touch the surface of the water. When they feel the water move a certain way, they know that prey is nearby and get ready to attack. This fishing spider has caught a small fish for a tasty meal.

4

The Fishing Spider's Family

Fishing spiders belong to a family called **Pisauridae**. They belong to a **genus**, or group, of pisaurids called *Dolomedes*. Spiders in the Pisauridae family are also known as nursery web weavers, because they weave a special web in which their babies live when they are born. There are more than 500 **species** in the Pisauridae family. They live in many different kinds of places. They can live in the jungles of South America and Africa, and on the edges of cold lakes in Siberia and Canada. They can live near the sea, a pond, or a stream. Most fishing spiders do not spin a web to catch their prey. They prefer to run after their prey on land or on the water. However, not all Pisauridae live near water. A few species of Pisauridae weave webs in trees or between rocks and hunt in the webs.

This fishing spider has caught a blue damselfly for its meal. It belongs to a genus of Pisauridae called Dolomedes. *There are 100 species of Pisauridae that only belong to the fishing spiders group.*

The Fishing Spider's Body

Spiders have two main body parts. The eyes, jaws, and legs are attached to the **cephalothorax**, or head. The rear part of the body, the **abdomen**, contains the spider's silk **glands**. Many fishing spiders have either long stripes that run along their sides or black and white spots on their bodies. Fishing spiders can be gray or brown, with brown or white legs. Their bodies are usually from 4 to 6 inches (10.1–15.2 cm) long. Their legspan is about 3 inches (7.6 cm). In most species of fishing spider, the female is bigger than the male.

(Top) This fishing spider has just molted. Its skin hangs from the branch. (Bottom) Notice the stripes on this fishing spider's abdomen.

Walking on Water

People can't walk on water because they are too heavy. Their feet would sink through the water's surface. However, spiders are light. An adult fishing spider weighs less than .06 ounce (1.7 g). At that weight, the **surface tension** of the water is strong enough to hold up the spider. Special hairs on the tips of the spider's feet help to spread the spider's weight. The spider's foot stretches the surface of the water like a sheet of rubber.

Fishing spiders can move across water in different ways. They use their four rear legs like the oars of a boat to push backward. They also use six of their legs to move quickly across the surface of the water by running and jumping a little bit at a time. They can sail across the water's surface by raising their body to catch the wind for a ride. Fishing spiders can also float on top of leaves.

This fishing spider is on top of a floating leaf. It waits for prey. Fishing spiders can jump off the surface of the water. They can jump 1 ½ inches (3.8 cm) straight up.

Spider Bites

Spiders don't eat the same way we do. They squirt a venomous liquid into their prey which turns the prey's insides into mush. Then they drink the soupy insides and leave the outer skin and the bones behind.

How Fishing Spiders Hunt

Fishing spiders can kill and eat animals that are bigger than they are. When fishing spiders hunt, they hide from their prey. They can feel prey walking on the water nearby or swimming just below the surface. Fishing spiders have good vision. When fishing spiders see prey that they want to eat, they run after the animal and grab it with all their legs. Then they bite the animal with their **fangs**. The **venom** in their bite **paralyzes** the prey. The spider drags the animal to the shore or to another safe spot to eat.

This reed frog and fish do not stand a chance of escaping. These fishing spiders will paralyze their prey with their venomous bites.

Spinning Silk

Unlike most spiders, fishing spiders do not spin webs to trap their prey. However, they do make a lot of different kinds of webs, such as draglines. Draglines are single strands of silk that fishing spiders attach to the shore, a leaf, or a plant. They use draglines to pull themselves back to safety if they get carried out too far into the water.

Female spiders use their silk to make a **protective** sac for their eggs. The web for which fishing spiders are most famous is their nursery web. The female spider makes the nursery web just before her eggs hatch. The nursery web is like a tent. The female spider weaves silk, leaves, and plant stems together to make a safe home for the baby spiders.

A female fishing spider has built a nest for her eggs. Notice the blades of grass that she used to make her nursery web.

The Fishing Spider's Eggs

To find a **mate**, a male fishing spider looks for the dragline of a female fishing spider. He can tell whether or not she is ready to mate by the way her dragline smells. Some female fishing spiders kill the males and eat them! This is why some male fishing spiders bring food to a female. This gives a male spider a chance to mate with the female while she eats. After mating, the female lays her eggs and makes an egg sac from silk to protect them. She carries the egg sac in her jaws for nearly a month, until the eggs are almost ready to hatch.

This female fishing spider carefully guards her egg sac from animals that prey upon eggs.

egg sac

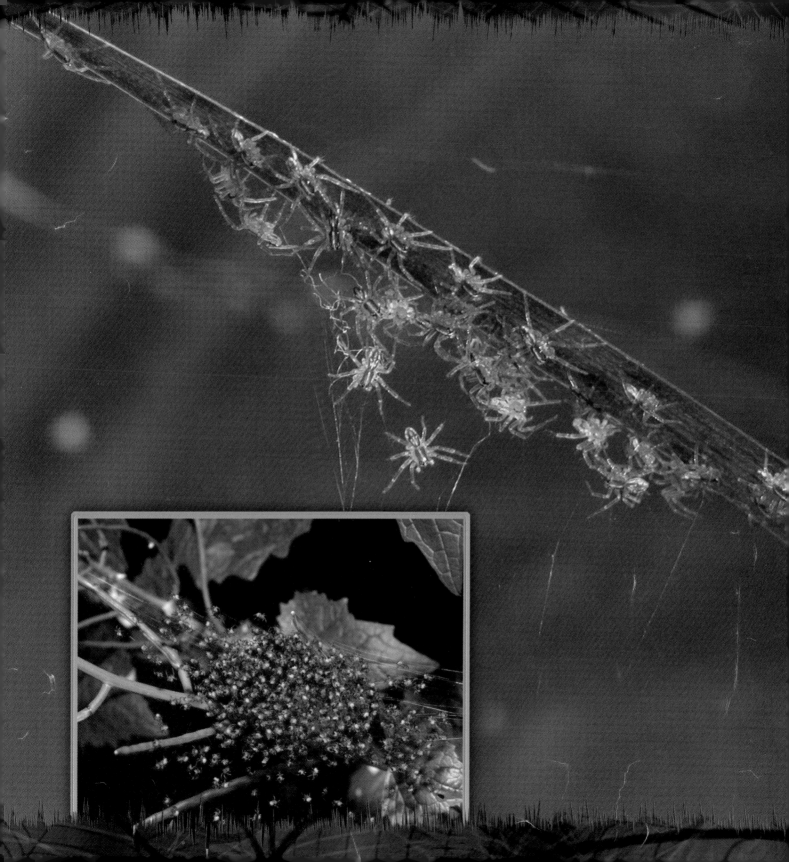

Baby Fishing Spiders

When the eggs are almost ready to hatch, the female fishing spider attaches the egg sac to a leaf or a plant stem. She spins the nursery web around the egg sac and waits for her babies to hatch. Depending on the species, there can be 100 baby spiders, or more than 1,000. The baby spiders are tiny. Their bodies are about 1/16 inch (2 mm) long. The mother stands guard until the babies are ready to go into the world. If she senses danger, she taps the nursery web with her foot to warn the baby spiders. After about one week, the young spiders leave the nursery. While they are still small, fishing spiders hunt from the tops of grasses and plants near the water's edge. They eat flies, mosquitoes, and young spiders.

Baby spiders are called spiderlings. Tiny spiderlings are crawling on a blade of grass. (Inset) These are baby fishing spiders in their nursery web. Sometimes fishing spiderlings will climb on top of their mother's back, which makes it look as if the mother spider is giving her spiderlings a piggyback ride!

The Fishing Spider's Enemies

Animals such as frogs, birds, and fish prey upon fishing spiders. Fishing spiders protect themselves by running away or hiding. They hide where there are a lot of plants. They may run down a plant stem under the water to get away from frogs and birds that hunt them at the water's surface. Fishing spiders can stay hidden underwater for more than half an hour. They breathe air that is trapped in bubbles around the hairs on their body. To get away from a fish, fishing spiders climb up a plant stem onto dry land or onto the top of a leaf or a dock.

Birds such as the snowy egret like to eat fishing spiders.

Fishing Spiders and People

People are scared of fishing spiders because they are big and hairy. However, people are more dangerous to fishing spiders than fishing spiders are to people. When people move to areas with swamps and other **wetlands** to farm or to build houses, they destroy fishing spiders' **habitat**.

Fishing spiders are shy of people. They would rather run away from people than bite them. Fishing spiders bite people only to defend eggs or to defend themselves. Luckily, a fishing spider looks more dangerous than it is. Its bite may hurt like a sting from a bee or a wasp, but it is not dangerous to a person unless the person is **allergic** to spider venom. As are most spiders, fishing spiders are good to have around because they eat a lot of insects that are annoying and unhealthy for people, such as mosquitoes.

Glossary

abdomen (AB-duh-min) The large, rear section of an insect's or a spider's body.

allergic (uh-LER-jik) Having a bad reaction to something.

cephalothorax (sef-uh-loh-THOR-aks) A spider's smaller, front body part, containing its head.

Dolomedes (DOH-luh-mee-dees) The genus of spiders to which fishing spiders belong.

fangs (FANGZ) Sharp, hollow or grooved teeth that inject venom.

genus (JEE-nuhs) The scientific name for a group of plants or animals that are alike. Members of the same genus are also members of the same family.

glands (GLANDZ) Organs or parts of the body that produce elements to help with bodily functions.

habitat (HA-bih-tat) The surroundings where an animal or a plant naturally lives.

mate (MAYT) A partner for making babies.

paralyzes (PAR-uh-lyz-ez) Causes to lose feeling or movement in the limbs.

Pisauridae (PIH-sor-ih-day) The family of spiders to which fishing spiders belong.

prey (PRAY) An animal that is hunted by another animal for food.

protective (pruh-TEK-tiv) Keeping from harm.

species (SPEE-sheez) A single kind of plant or animal. All people are one species.

surface tension (SER-fis TEN-chun) The force that holds the surface of a liquid together.

tadpoles (TAD-pohlz) Baby frogs or toads that look like fish and live under the water.

venom (VEH-num) A poison passed by one animal into another through a bite or sting.

wetlands (WET-lands) Shallow, marshy areas near rivers and oceans where many water creatures live.

Index

A
abdomen, 8

B
baby spiders, 15
birds, 20

C
Canada, 7

D
Dolomedes, 7
dragline(s), 15–16

E
eggs, 15–16, 19, 22
egg sac, 16, 19

H
habitat, 22

M
mate, 16

N
nursery web, 7, 15, 19

P
Pisauridae, 7
prey, 4, 7, 12, 15

S
Siberia, 7
South America, 7

V
venom, 12, 22

W
wetlands, 22

Web Sites

Due to the changing nature of Internet links, PowerKids Press has developed an online list of Web sites related to the subject of this book. This site is updated regularly. Please use this link to access the list: www.powerkidslinks.com/lspi/fishing/